MOM'S HAVING A BABY

CAN I TRADE FOR A PONY?

by Stephanie Houtchen

Illustrations by Stephanie Houtchen

AF483751

Dedicated to all my grandchildren.
You're all such a blessing and
I love you!

Mom's having a baby,
and all I have to say,

"Can I trade for a pony?"
They both said, "NO WAY!"

Mom sits on the couch resting,
I can see her stomach roll.

She puts my hand on her belly,
he kicks me with his toes.

My parents say it doesn't matter,
their love for me won't change.

But they say I'll have to share;
my room will be rearranged.

I bet he'll grab all my best cars

and even my
biggest toy gun.

I'll probably have to babysit.

This is not going to be any fun!

I'm sure he'll try to scribble in my best coloring book.

I know I can't be rough
with him,
but I can give my
meanest look.

Mom
wants me
to help
feed him,

and get
him
dressed
for bed.

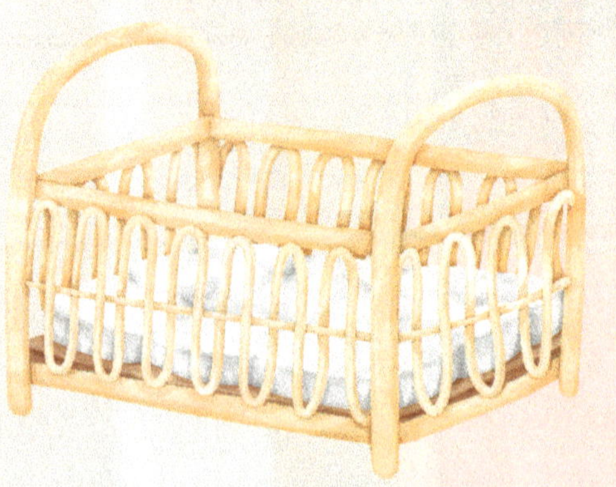

But I won't change
his diaper;
can't picture
that
in my head.

Dad says I can
teach him

how to play ball

or ride a bike.

I think I would
rather
show him
how to take a hike.

When I woke up
this morning,
Dad was rushing
to get me dressed.

I asked
him where
Mom was,
he just said,
"We
have
a
new guest."

He drove us to the hospital,

We rode up
to the baby floor.

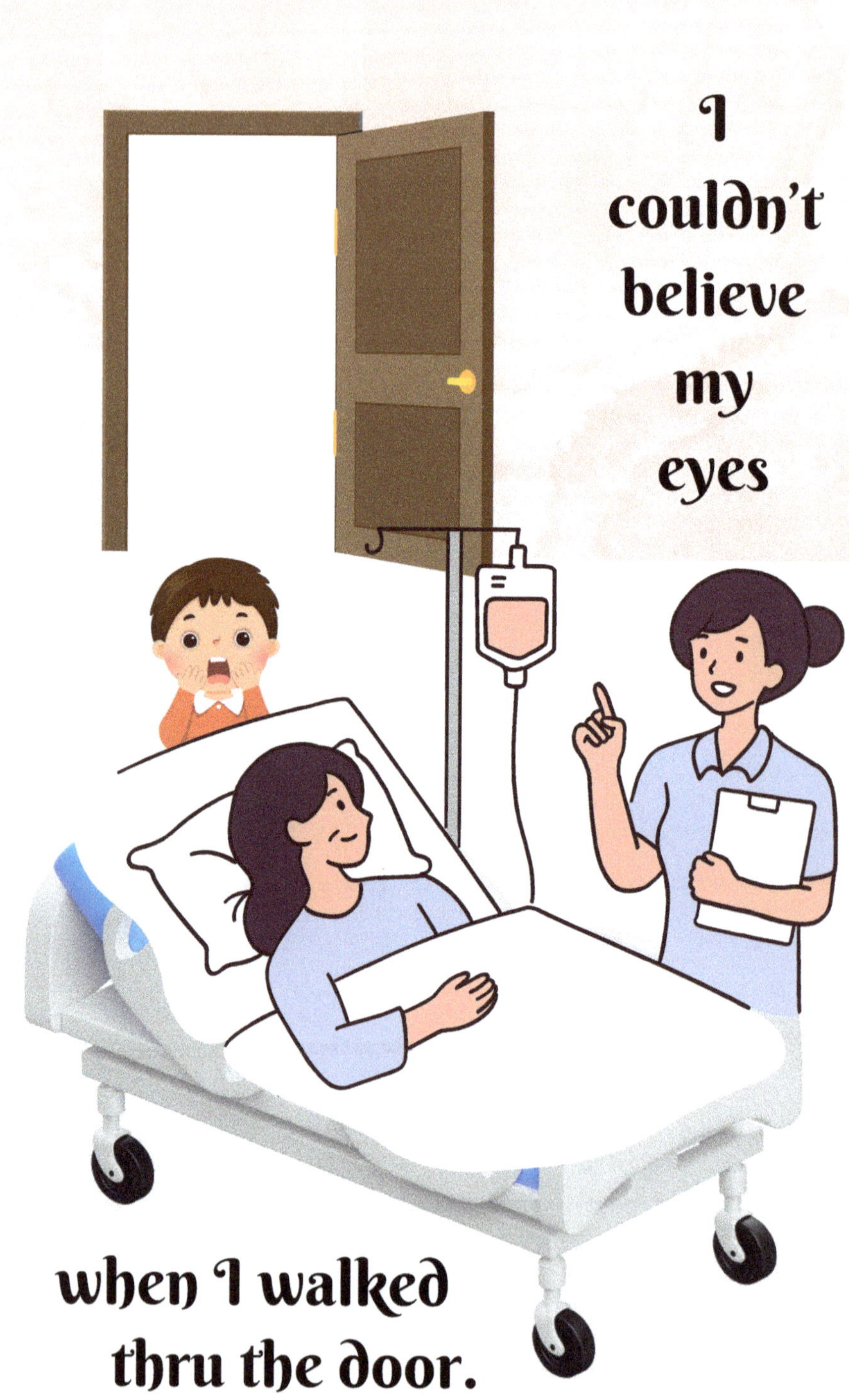

I couldn't believe my eyes
when I walked thru the door.

A GIRL!!

A FEMALE!!

A SISTER!!

Hmmm....
I think she looks like me.

Dad laid her
in my arms;
rested her
bottom on
my knee.

Now this really
changes things,
a sister could
be pretty cool.
She won't want
to play with
my toys;
boy have
I been a fool.

We'll have to get her some dolls,

**and bows for her
light brown hair.**

The two of us
together
will make such a
wonderful pair.

I have a new baby sister, and she's as sweet as honey.

I wouldn't trade her for ANYTHING!

Not even
a pony!

About Stephanie Houtchen

Stephanie Houtchen, with husband Michael, has five children, eleven grandchildren, and loves writing children's books and poetry. She wrote her first children's book when she retired in 2014. She loves to read and can be dangerous with knitting needles when she's not playing with her grandchildren.

Copyright © 2024 by Stephanie Houtchen

All rights reserved. No portion of this book may be copied or transmitted in any form, electronic or otherwise, without express written consent of the publisher or author.

Cover copyright © 2024 Seventh Star Press, LLC.

Illustrations: Stephanie Houtchen

Editor: Holly Phillippe

Published by Seventh StarChild

ISBN: 979-8-3481-6057-9

Seventh StarChild is an imprint of Seventh Star Press

www.seventhstarpress.com

info@seventhstarpress.com

Publisher's Note:

Mom's Having a Baby is a work of fiction. All names, characters, and places are the product of the author's imagination, used in fictitious manner. Any resemblances to actual persons, places, locales, events, etc. are purely coincidental.

Printed in the United States of America

First Edition

www.ingramcontent.com/pod-product-compliance
Lightning Source LLC
Chambersburg PA
CBHW040117150726
48005CB00013B/1759